BEAVER BOOKS

My First Bilingual Book · Mon premier livre bilingue

Zoo Animals

Les animaux du zoo

English-French · Français-anglais

— A child's first book of words and fun – in two languages! —
— Un livre bilingue, rempli de mots et de plaisir pour les tout-petits! —

bear

un ours

elephant

un éléphant

giraffe

une girafe

monkey

un singe

crocodile

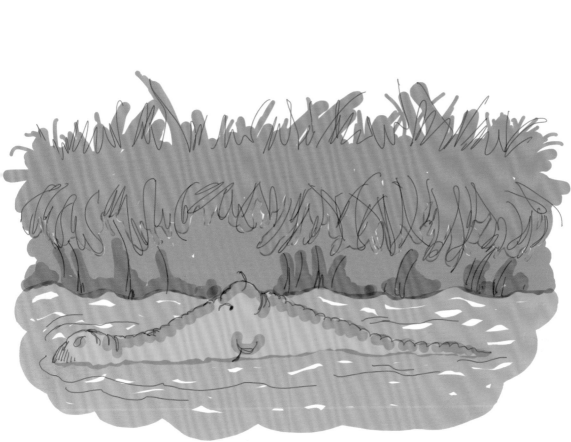

un crocodile

zebra

un zèbre

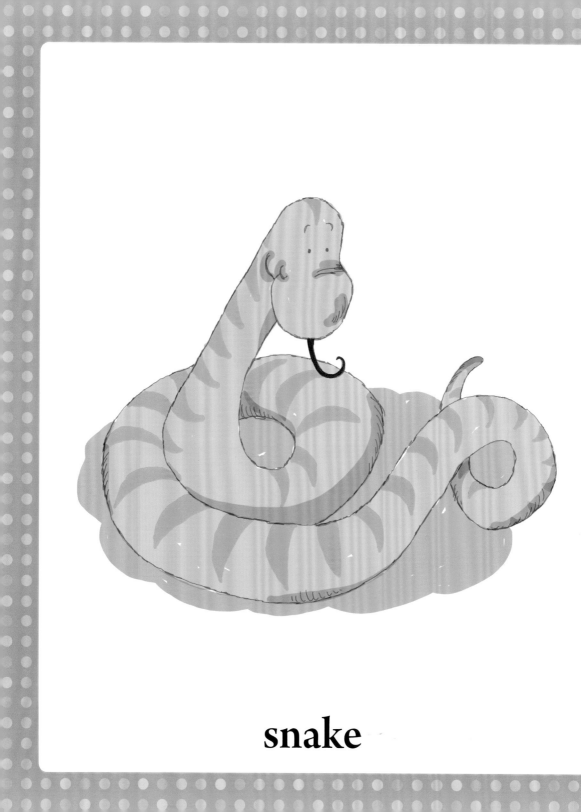

snake

un serpent

lion

un lion

koala

un koala

kangaroo

un kangourou

hippopotamus

un hippopotame

— Fun activities with animal names! —
— Des activités amusantes! —

Can you say the names of these animals in French and English?
Nomme en français et en anglais tous les animaux qui sont présentés ici.

Say the animal name and find its picture in the book.

Prononce les mots que tu vois ici et
retrouve les animaux correspondants dans le livre.

kangaroo	**crocodile**	**hippopotamus**	**koala**
un kangourou	**un crocodile**	**un hippopotame**	**un koala**